D1498218

IF YOU WERE A KID BUILDING A
Pyramid

BY LAWRENCE SCHIMEL • ILLUSTRATED BY JENNIFER ELY

CHILDREN'S PRESS® An Imprint of Scholastic Inc.

Content Consultant
Emily Teeter, PhD, Research Associate, The Oriental Institute of the University of Chicago

NOTE TO THE READER, PARENT, LIBRARIAN, AND TEACHER: This book combines a historical fiction
narrative with nonfiction fact boxes. While all the nonfiction fact boxes are historically accurate
and true, the fiction comes solely from the imaginations of the author and illustrator.

Photos ©: 9: Cultura RM Exclusive/Seth K. Hughes/Getty Images; 11: PRISMA ARCHIVO/Alamy Images; 13: dieKleinert/Alamy
Images; 15: Reinhard Dirscherl/age fotostock; 17: Patrick Landmann/Getty Images; 19: Peter Unger/Getty Images; 21 right: DEA/G.
DAGLI ORTI/The Granger Collection; 21 center: DEA/G. DAGLI ORTI/The Granger Collection; 21 left: DEA/G. DAGLI ORTI/The
Granger Collection; 23: Patrick CHAPUIS/Gamma-Rapho/Getty Images; 25: Tibor Bognár/age fotostock; 27: cinoby/iStockphoto.

Library of Congress Cataloging-in-Publication Data
Names: Schimel, Lawrence, author. | Ely, Jennifer, illustrator.
Title: If you were a kid building a pyramid / by Lawrence Schimel ; illustrated by Jennifer Ely.
Other titles: If you were a kid.
Description: New York, NY : Children's Press, an imprint of Scholastic Inc., [2017] | Series: If you were a kid |
Includes bibliographical references and index.
Identifiers: LCCN 2017011862 | ISBN 9780531237489 (library binding) | ISBN 9780531239490 (pbk.)
Subjects: LCSH: Pyramids—Juvenile literature. | Egypt—Civilization—To 332
B.C.—Juvenile literature. | Egypt—Social life and customs—To 332 B.C.—Juvenile literature.
Classification: LCC DT63 .S33 2017 | DDC 932—dc23
LC record available at https://lccn.loc.gov/2017011862

No part of this publication may be reproduced in whole or in part, or stored in a retrieval system, or transmitted in any form or by any
means, electronic, mechanical, photocopying, recording, or otherwise, without written permission of the publisher. For information regarding
permission, write to Scholastic Inc., Attention: Permissions Department, 557 Broadway, New York, NY 10012.
© 2018 Scholastic Inc.

All rights reserved. Published in 2018 by Children's Press, an imprint of Scholastic Inc.
Printed in the United States of America 113

SCHOLASTIC, CHILDREN'S PRESS, and associated logos are trademarks and/or registered trademarks of
Scholastic Inc., 557 Broadway, New York, NY 10012.

1 2 3 4 5 6 7 8 9 10 R 27 26 25 24 23 22 21 20 19 18

TABLE OF CONTENTS

A Different Way of Life

Thousands of years ago, ancient Egypt was one of the world's greatest civilizations. It was ruled by a series of **pharaohs**, or kings. The people of Egypt believed that the pharaohs had a special connection to their gods. They also believed that the pharaohs' spirits lived on after death. To provide a lasting home for these spirits, they built huge structures called pyramids. When a pharaoh died, his body was sealed inside a pyramid.

Imagine you were a kid in ancient Egypt. The building of pyramids would be among the most important events that took place during your lifetime. If you had the opportunity to help with the construction, it would not only be a job. It would also be an honor.

Turn the page to visit this amazing time in ancient history! You will see that life today is a lot different than it was in the past.

Meet Seneb!

This is Seneb. He is a teenage boy living in Egypt in the 2500s BCE. His father works making clay pots. Seneb works as his **apprentice**. He likes working with clay, but sometimes he dreams of a more exciting life. He wishes he could explore the pyramid that is being built for the pharaoh. But Seneb's father can't do his work alone. Sometimes Seneb is jealous of his neighbor Merti, who gets to spend her time exploring with her younger brother . . .

Meet Merti!

This is Merti. She lives with her family near the Nile River. She is very responsible. Her job is to watch over her younger brother Sabu, so their mother can take care of their new baby brother. But she wishes she were allowed to do something more interesting. Sometimes she is jealous of her neighbor Seneb, who will one day get to take over his father's pottery studio. Merti still doesn't know what she will do when she grows up . . .

"You're getting taller every day, it seems!" said Seneb's mother, measuring him against the height marker in the doorway. "You're almost a man!"

Through the door, Seneb could see the pyramid that was already nearing completion. He wondered if he would get a chance to see inside it before it was finished.

"I'm growing faster than the pyramid!" Seneb replied with a smile.

AN ENORMOUS WORKFORCE

Many of the details of the pyramids' construction remain a mystery even today. It was once believed that they were built by slaves. However, newer evidence indicates that each one was made by about 10,000 skilled workers. These laborers worked in shifts to finish building as quickly as possible. Each pyramid had to be finished within the period of a pharaoh's reign.

Building a pyramid could take about 20 years.

Merti held up her hand to block the sunlight from her eyes. Every day, she took Sabu down to the riverbank so he could watch as groups of very strong men unloaded enormous stones from the boats. But she was starting to get bored of visiting the same place over and over. She was almost an adult now. When would she be allowed to have her own life instead of spending every day with her little brother?

THE LONG HAUL

Each pyramid was built from a huge number of stone blocks. Limestone and granite were the most common kinds. Where did all those stones come from? First they were dug up from **quarries**.

Then they were dragged to the construction site. Special types of stone, like granite, were brought from hundreds of miles away. The journey took up to 20 days!

Each of these enormous limestone blocks weighed about 5,000 pounds (2,268 kilograms).

Seneb carried a large jar to the river to bring water back to the pottery studio. He saw Merti and Sabu and waved hello. Just then, there was a loud cry of pain from behind them. Many of the men who were unloading the blocks began shouting. Merti, Sabu, and Seneb exchanged glances and ran toward the crowd of people.

"Look! That man's hand was crushed under the stone," Sabu cried.

Seneb felt sorry for the man. But he also started to get an idea.

HEAVY LIFTING

The ancient Egyptians relied on human strength to move the heavy blocks of stone. It is thought that the stones were dragged on wooden sleds over wet sand for easier movement. It is also possible that teams of workers pushed or pulled the stones using wooden logs as rollers.

Workers pull a stone block using a wooden sled.

Seneb asked Merti if she was busy that day.

"Just taking care of Sabu," she replied.

"Do you want to take my place in the pottery studio for the day?" Seneb asked. "I'm going to volunteer to take that injured man's place."

"Won't that be dangerous?" Merti asked.

"Maybe," Seneb answered. "But this is my chance to see inside the pyramid!"

STUDYING THE PAST

The study of ancient human history is called **archaeology**. Archaeologists study the pyramids and the surrounding areas very closely to learn what life was like for people in ancient Egypt. They also do their best to figure out exactly how the pyramids were built. This isn't always easy. Even after many years of careful study, there are still things left to learn about the pyramids and ancient Egypt.

Archaeologists make careful notes about the things they discover in pyramids and at other ancient sites.

"I want to go to the pyramid with Seneb!" Sabu said.

"Maybe when you're older," Merti replied.

Sabu followed Merti as she carried Seneb's jar of water back to the pottery studio. It was very heavy. She had to stop often to rest. But she was excited. Today she wasn't just a babysitter! Maybe she would even help make something that could be used by the pyramid builders. That would be an honor!

GETTING READY
FOR THE AFTERLIFE

Mummification preserved the bodies of the pharaohs, their families, and other high-ranking people. This process involved drying out the bodies. This was done using chemicals. Organs such as the stomach and lungs were removed from the body and stored in special jars.

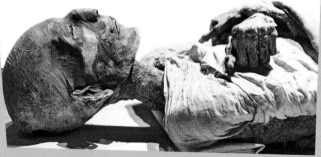

The mummy of an ancient Egyptian pharaoh on display at a museum in Egypt

Seneb soon learned that it wasn't easy to move a block of stone that was taller than he was. But working together with the other laborers, he was able to push it forward little by little. It was almost like magic! Seneb matched his movements to the man beside him. Together, they took one step after another. Before long, they reached the pyramid itself.

RAMPS AND LEVERS

There are many theories explaining how the stones of the pyramids were raised into place. Most suggest that ramps were used. The ramps rose higher as each stone layer was added. They were then taken apart after construction was completed. It is also thought that wooden levers were used to help lift the stones. This theory is often used to explain the construction of the upper portions of the pyramids.

The biggest pyramids are as tall as skyscrapers.

Seneb's father was surprised when Merti and Sabu arrived at the studio instead of his son. But he allowed them to work with him that day.

Sabu soon lost interest in making pots. "Let's go back to the river!" he begged.

But Merti loved being surrounded by the tools and half-finished pots in the studio. Even though the work was messy, she was happy. She felt like she was doing something useful at last!

EVERYDAY OBJECTS

The **artifacts** found in the ruins of ancient places can tell us a lot about the past. Even simple objects like clay pots and jars can help us understand what life was like for ancient people. Sometimes archaeological discoveries have changed the way we think about past events. For instance, the discovery of workers' camps showed that the pyramids were likely built by skilled laborers and not slaves.

Ancient Egyptian artifacts

Sandals

Comb

Bowl

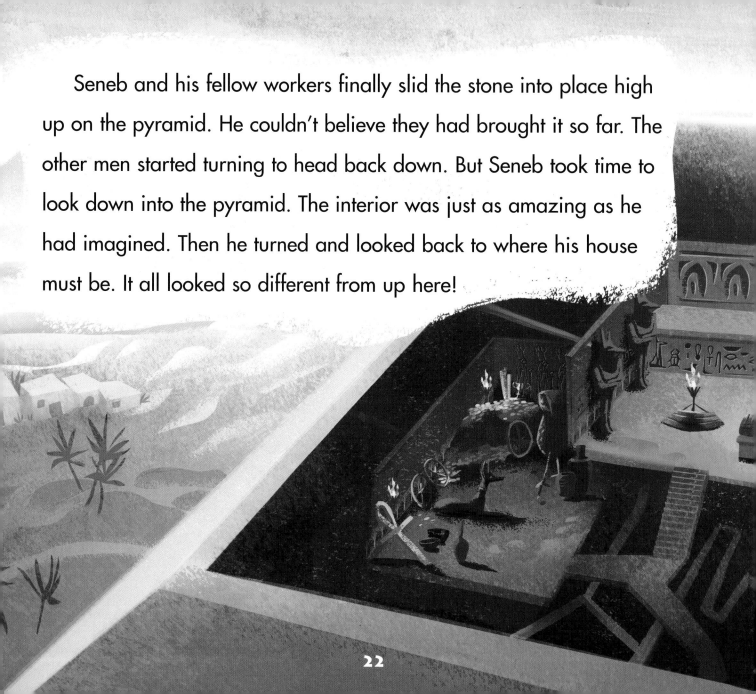

Seneb and his fellow workers finally slid the stone into place high up on the pyramid. He couldn't believe they had brought it so far. The other men started turning to head back down. But Seneb took time to look down into the pyramid. The interior was just as amazing as he had imagined. Then he turned and looked back to where his house must be. It all looked so different from up here!

WHAT'S INSIDE?

The pyramids are large enough to have space for many rooms inside. However, they are mostly solid. Most contain just a few rooms. The largest one is for the pharaoh. The rooms are connected with various narrow passages and ramps. Some rooms were also hidden behind false walls to trick tomb robbers!

Some pyramid passages are too narrow for people to stand in.

23

The next morning, Merti and Sabu waited for Seneb by the riverside. At last, he came down to fetch water.

"There he is!" Sabu cried.

"We were worried something had happened to you," Merti said.

"I'm fine," Seneb replied. "I'm just tired. My whole body is sore!"

"In that case, we'll help you carry the water," Merti offered.

"What was the pyramid like?" Sabu asked.

DIFFERENT ERAS, DIFFERENT STYLES

Pyramids built during different times have different shapes. For example, the oldest known Egyptian pyramid was built between 2667 BCE and 2648 BCE. It is what's known as a step pyramid. This means the sides look like stairs. The Great Pyramid of Giza was built in the 2500s BCE in Egypt. It is what's called a true pyramid. This means its four sides are smooth triangles.

The Pyramid of Djoser is the most famous step pyramid.

"It was one of the most amazing things I've ever seen," Seneb said. "I'm proud that I got to be a part of building it. Now I know why it is taking so long to build. I'll be an adult before it's finished."

"Not all pyramids take so long to build," Merti said. "I made this one in no time at all." She held out a tiny clay pyramid in her hand. "It's for you, Sabu!"

Everyone laughed as they entered the pottery studio.

OTHER PYRAMIDS

The ancient Egyptians were not the only people to build pyramids. Different versions of these amazing structures can be found all over the world. Sometimes they were religious sites. Other times they were simply buildings for everyday use. Some of the most famous pyramids were built by the Aztec and Mayan people in Central and South America.

A famous ancient Mayan pyramid can be found at Chichén Itzá in Mexico.

Ancient Egyptian Landmarks

Pyramids of Giza
This site is home to three major pyramids as well as several other ancient structures.

Nile Delta

Sphinx
This giant statue in Giza has the body of a lion and the head of a man.

Pyramid of Djoser
This step pyramid stands more than 200 feet (61 meters) tall.

Memphis
This ancient city was founded more than 5,000 years ago.

Nile River

Stone Quarry
Ancient Egyptians had to transport stone blocks from the quarry to pyramid construction sites.

Timeline

2667–2648 BCE   The earliest pyramid is built by the architect Imhotep for Pharaoh Djoser.

2589–2566 BCE   The Great Pyramid of Giza, the largest and perhaps the most famous pyramid in the world, is built during the reign of Pharaoh Khufu.

2278–2184 BCE   The last of the great pyramids is built in Saqqara for Pharaoh Pepi II.

2011 CE   Using a small robot, archaeologists explore a part of the Great Pyramid's interior that has not been visited by humans in 4,500 years.

Words to Know

apprentice (uh-PREN-tiss) someone who learns a skill by working with an expert

archaeology (ahr-kee-AH-luh-jee) the study of the past, which often involves digging up old buildings, objects, and bones and examining them carefully

artifacts (AHR-tuh-fakts) objects made or changed by human beings, especially tools or weapons used in the past

mummification (muhm-uh-fuh-KAY-shuhn) the process of preserving a dead body with special chemicals and then wrapping it in cloth

pharaohs (FAIR-ohz) titles given to kings in ancient Egypt

quarries (KWOR-eez) places where stone, slate, or sand is dug from the ground

Index

ABOUT THE AUTHOR

Lawrence Schimel is an award-winning author who writes in both Spanish and English. He has published over 50 books for kids. He lives in Madrid, Spain, where in addition to his own writing, he works as a literary translator.

ABOUT THE ILLUSTRATOR

Jenn Ely loves stories! As a child, she spent a lot of time doodling characters from her favorite tales. As an adult, not much has changed. She spends her days in her home studio in Portland, Oregon, designing worlds for various animated films, television shows, and the occasional book.

Visit this Scholastic website for more information about pyramids:

www.factsfornow.scholastic.com
Enter the keyword **Pyramid**

32

CCPY4004760915